Space

Louie Stowell

Designed by Anna Gould

Illustrated by John Fox and Adrian Roots
Picture strips by Paul Davidson

Space expert consultant: Stuart Atkinson

Russian craft expert: Anatoly Zak

Dragon spacecraft flying
above Earth connected
to a robot arm

Contents

Astronauts working on the *International Space Station*

3

Launching into space

For the past 70 years or so, vehicles have been flying into space — the vast, airless region beyond our planet and its atmosphere. Most spacecraft are launched into space using a type of rocket known as a launch vehicle.

Ariane V (launch vehicle)

(Europe, 1996–present)

- **Purpose:** carries a spacecraft inside its nose during launch then releases the craft and falls away.

This is a type of launch vehicle known as an Ariane V. Part of the illustration has been cut away to show where the spacecraft is stored during launch.

Booster rocket: helps the main engine to lift the launch vehicle off the ground. There is a booster on each side of the main fuel tank.

Fuel tank for main engine

Exhaust nozzle

Main rocket engine

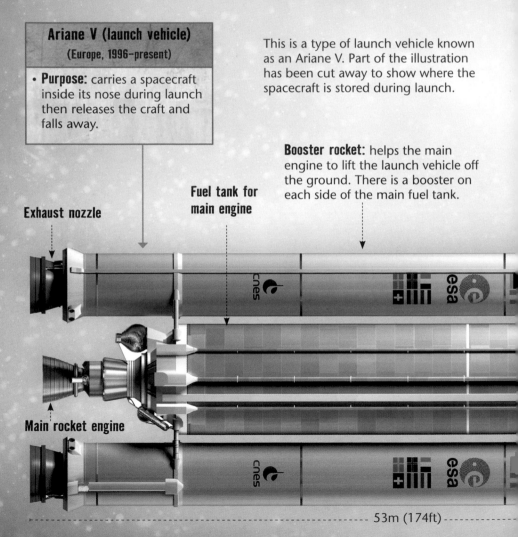

53m (174ft)

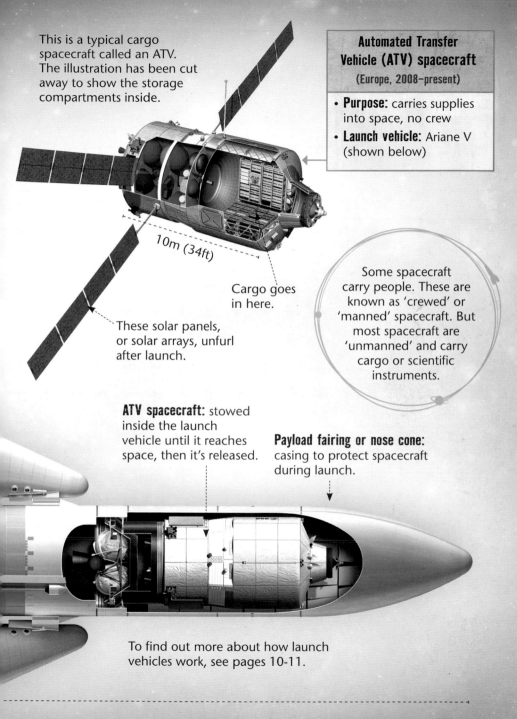

This is a typical cargo spacecraft called an ATV. The illustration has been cut away to show the storage compartments inside.

Automated Transfer Vehicle (ATV) spacecraft
(Europe, 2008–present)

- **Purpose:** carries supplies into space, no crew
- **Launch vehicle:** Ariane V (shown below)

10m (34ft)

Cargo goes in here.

These solar panels, or solar arrays, unfurl after launch.

Some spacecraft carry people. These are known as 'crewed' or 'manned' spacecraft. But most spacecraft are 'unmanned' and carry cargo or scientific instruments.

ATV spacecraft: stowed inside the launch vehicle until it reaches space, then it's released.

Payload fairing or nose cone: casing to protect spacecraft during launch.

To find out more about how launch vehicles work, see pages 10-11.

Space explorers

Over 500 people from nearly 40 countries have flown into space.

Who goes into space?

Astronauts: professional space voyagers who are often trained scientists. Astronauts who work for the Russian government are known as **cosmonauts**. Chinese astronauts are sometimes referred to as **taikonauts** or **yuhangyuans**.

Space tourists: people who pay to take a trip into space.

Robots: most space exploration is done by robots, not humans. (Find out more on pages 34-41.)

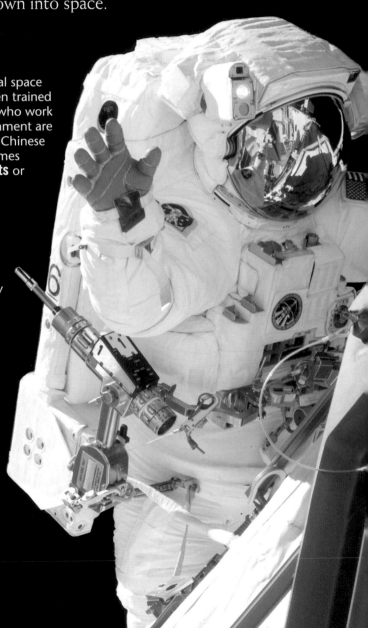

This American astronaut is wearing a spacesuit called an EMU. (For more about spacesuits, see pages 26-27.)

Why go into space?

Because it's there. Humans love to explore the unknown, whether it's a high mountain or an alien planet. But each journey into space, or space mission, is an opportunity to make new scientific and technological discoveries.

Who do astronauts work for?

Most astronauts or cosmonauts work for their country or continent's space agency, although private companies are starting to fly their own spacecraft too. Here are the main space agencies.

National Aeronautics and Space Administration (NASA), the United States' space agency

Canadian Space Agency (CSA)

European Space Agency (ESA)

Russian Federal Space Agency (RFSA), also known as Roskosmos

Indian Space Research Organisation (ISRO)

China National Space Administration (CNSA)

Japan Aerospace Exploration Agency (JAXA)

Where is outer space?

There's a layer of gas around our planet called the atmosphere. It gets thinner and thinner, fading into nothing. That's where outer space, or space, begins.

Planes fly about 9km (5.5 miles) up.

Once you get 100km (62 miles) up, most scientists agree that you're in outer space. This is known as the **Karman Line**.

Spy planes fly at heights of around 23km (14.2 miles).

Cheating gravity

Gravity is the force that keeps you from floating into the air when you're on Earth.

To reach space, a launch vehicle has to fight against the mighty pull of Earth's gravity. (Find out how it does that on pages 10-11.)

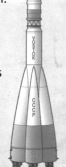

Outer space is a vacuum. That means there's no air or other gases, and hardly any matter (stuff) of any type at all.

8

The Solar System

Earth is one of eight planets circling around, or orbiting, the Sun. The Sun and all the objects in orbit around it make up the Solar System.

This illustration is based on data from NASA spacecraft. The planets have been squeezed closer together to fit on the page.

The Sun

Earth

- **Type:** terrestrial, meaning rocky
- **Atmosphere:** thick, breathable
- **Key fact:** abundant water allowed life to develop (this means you).

Mercury

- **Type:** terrestrial, meaning rocky
- **Atmosphere:** none
- **Key fact:** the smallest planet orbiting the Sun

Mars

- **Type:** terrestrial, meaning rocky
- **Atmosphere:** very thin
- **Key fact:** spacecraft have discovered evidence of water on its surface.

Venus

- **Type:** terrestrial, meaning rocky
- **Atmosphere:** very thick, not breathable
- **Key fact:** powerful acid in its atmosphere and crushing air pressure destroy any spacecraft trying to land on its surface.

Jupiter

- **Type:** gas giant: a giant planet made of gas, but with a rocky core. You can't land on a gas giant, because you'd sink in.
- **Atmosphere:** thick
- **Key fact:** largest planet in the Solar System

Ganymede

The Solar System contains many small objects called asteroids, made of rock and, sometimes, metal. Many of these orbit the Sun between Mars and Jupiter. This area is known as the Asteroid Belt.

Moons of the Solar System

- A moon is a rocky or, sometimes, icy object in orbit around a planet. Ours is known as the Moon.
- Mercury and Venus have no moons.
- Ganymede, the largest moon in the Solar System, orbits Jupiter.

Liftoff!

Flying in a curved path around a planet, star or moon, is known as being in **orbit**.

The Moon is in orbit around Earth, around 380,000 km (235,000 miles) away.

300 km
(186 miles)

200 km
(124 miles)

100 km
(62 miles)

The *International Space Station* (ISS) orbits about 354km (220 miles) up. Find out more on pages 18-25.

Before a launch there's usually a countdown lasting several hours, so safety checks can be performed. Just before zero, mighty rocket engines fire. We have liftoff!

This is a crewed Russian spacecraft known as a **Soyuz** and its launch vehicle, seconds after liftoff.

Nose cone containing spacecraft

Launch vehicle with multiple rocket engines

Burning exhaust fumes

How rocket engines work

Rocket engines burn fuel inside them which creates fiery exhaust fumes.

The fumes escape through a nozzle at the bottom, pushing against the ground and creating a force called thrust that lifts the rocket.

Fuel burns in here

Thrust

Exhaust

Space dangers

Outer space is full of dangers:

- **There's no air to breathe**
- **There is lots of killer radiation**
- **EXTREME temperatures**

Astronauts floating unprotected in space would die very quickly, so they need spacesuits and other equipment to keep them alive and safe.

Service tower, a support which pulls back at liftoff

Launch pad

9

Robot explorers

Humans have sent robot spacecraft called probes to the very edge of the Solar System and beyond.
Find out more about probes on pages 34-35.

A probe called *Voyager 1* is now on its way out of the Solar System.

Humans haven't visited any other planets. Astronauts have only flown as far as Earth's own Moon so far.

Uranus

- **Type**: ice giant: icy core surrounded by gases
- **Atmosphere**: thick
- **Key fact:** has rings like Saturn, but they're much fainter

Neptune

- **Type**: ice giant: icy core surrounded by gases
- **Atmosphere**: thick
- **Key fact:** has very wild weather in its atmosphere

Saturn

- **Type**: gas giant: a giant planet made of a mix of gases, but with a rocky core
- **Atmosphere**: thick
- **Key fact:** its rings are made of chunks of ice and rock

A space probe called *Cassini* is currently in orbit around Saturn.

When probes visited Uranus and Neptune, they showed that these planets have rings, too, although they're much smaller than Saturn's.

This is the Kuiper Belt. Like the Asteroid Belt, it is home to many asteroids orbiting the Sun. 'Dwarf planets' such as Pluto that are too small to be classed as proper planets are also found here.

Launch stages

During a launch, a series of rocket engines fires. Each engine or cluster of engines is known as a stage.

This is what happens during a typical **Soyuz** launch.

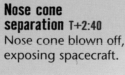

Third stage separation T+9:00
Third stage drops off, spacecraft flies solo in orbit and solar arrays are deployed.

Second stage separation T+4:58
Used-up second stage falls off and third stage rockets fire.

Nose cone separation T+2:40
Nose cone blown off, exposing spacecraft.

Into space T+1.58
First stage rockets detach and fall to Earth and the second stage keeps firing.

Launch pad T-2.30 to T-zero
During countdown, safety checks are performed, then the first and second stage engines fire.

Measuring time

During countdown, time is counted backwards from launch.

So T-2 hours means two hours before launch.

After launch, time is measured as T+ time passed since launch.

Soyuz spacecraft

This is a Soyuz, a type of Russian spacecraft used to ferry people to and from Earth's orbit. It has three main sections, known as 'modules'.

Soyuz spacecraft have been used since the late 1960s. This is a 2010 model.

Only this module returns to Earth.

Descent module: where crew sit for launch, re-entry and landing (see pages 32-33)

Orbital module: used by the crew while in orbit

СОЮЗ

Periscope: used by the crew to look outside the spacecraft

Docking mechanism: docking means connecting to another craft in space. Find out more about Soyuz's docking process on pages 20-21.

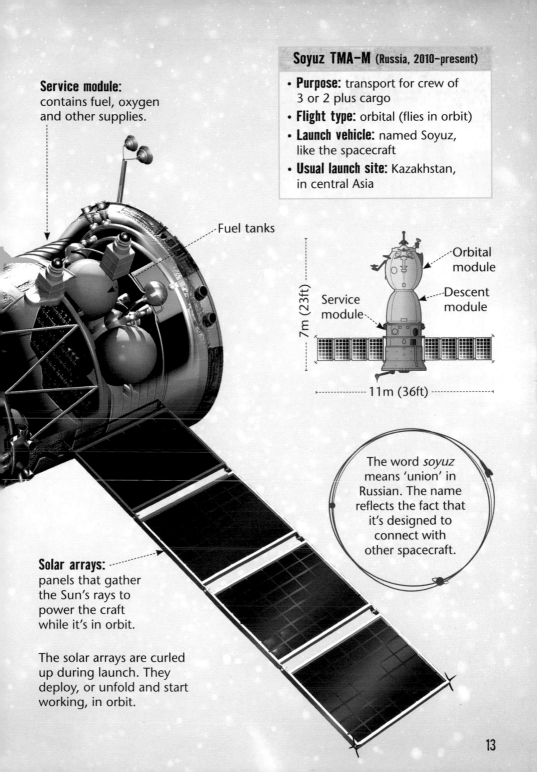

Service module:
contains fuel, oxygen
and other supplies.

Fuel tanks

Solar arrays:
panels that gather
the Sun's rays to
power the craft
while it's in orbit.

The solar arrays are curled
up during launch. They
deploy, or unfold and start
working, in orbit.

Soyuz TMA-M (Russia, 2010-present)

• **Purpose:** transport for crew of
  3 or 2 plus cargo
• **Flight type:** orbital (flies in orbit)
• **Launch vehicle:** named Soyuz,
  like the spacecraft
• **Usual launch site:** Kazakhstan,
  in central Asia

Orbital
module

Descent
module

Service
module

7m (23ft)

11m (36ft)

The word *soyuz*
means 'union' in
Russian. The name
reflects the fact that
it's designed to
connect with
other spacecraft.

Launch positions

During launch of a Soyuz spacecraft, the crew sits in the cramped descent module.

This diagram shows inside the descent module.

Hatch: leads to orbital module

Control panel: shows details of the flight's progress.

Video camera

Periscope: allows crew to look out and measure distances outside the craft

Window

Parachute hatch: where the parachutes come out during landing

Shock-absorbing seats

Engines: used for landing on the journey home

Flight engineer	Crew commander	Passenger
• Assists commander by reading out control panel data • Operates the radio and TV camera • Monitors life support	• Gives orders • Responsible for all vehicle operations and crew safety • Performs any manual controls necessary	• Could be a space tourist or a scientist • Not usually involved in flight processes

Flight suits

During liftoff and landing, astronauts and cosmonauts wear protective suits.

This NASA suit is nicknamed the pumpkin suit because it's bright, pumpkin orange.

Temperature-control underwear worn beneath suit

This cosmonaut is testing his made-to-measure seat lining. The seat will be fitted in the Soyuz descent module for launch and landing.

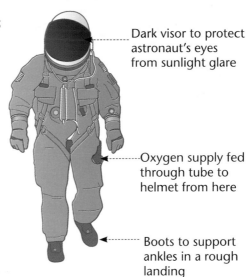

Dark visor to protect astronaut's eyes from sunlight glare

Oxygen supply fed through tube to helmet from here

Boots to support ankles in a rough landing

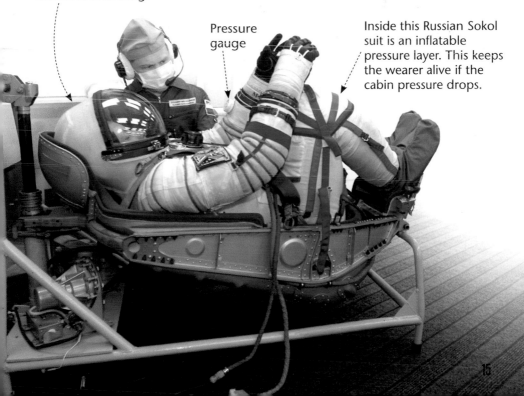

Pressure gauge

Inside this Russian Sokol suit is an inflatable pressure layer. This keeps the wearer alive if the cabin pressure drops.

This is NASA Mission Control during a Space Shuttle mission to the *International Space Station*. Find out more on pages 18-19 and 58-61.

Mission Control

Orders on a NASA mission come from Mission Control Center (MCC) in Houston, Texas. Most staff members are in charge of a specific aspect of the mission.

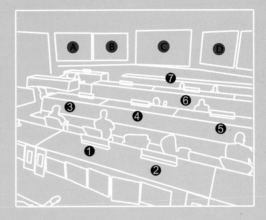

Seating chart

❶and ❷ Medical team: on hand to advise astronauts

❸Flight Director: in charge of the mission

❹CAPCOM: in charge of talking to the astronauts (only one person talks to them to avoid confusion.)

❺Trajectory operations (TOPO) officer: makes sure the craft is going in the right direction at the right speed.

❻Life support officer: monitors on-board air and water.

❼SPARTAN: staff members in charge of electrical power systems inside and outside the ISS.

What's on the screens?

Ⓐ Live camera feed from outside the ISS

Ⓑ Live feed from camera on station's robot arm

Ⓒ World map showing position of spacecraft

Ⓓ Cautions and warnings from the ISS computer

The ISS

The *International Space Station* (ISS) is a vast spacecraft in orbit around Earth. Crew members do scientific experiments there, making use of the unique conditions of outer space.

This photo was taken in 2011 by an astronaut leaving the ISS aboard a Soyuz.

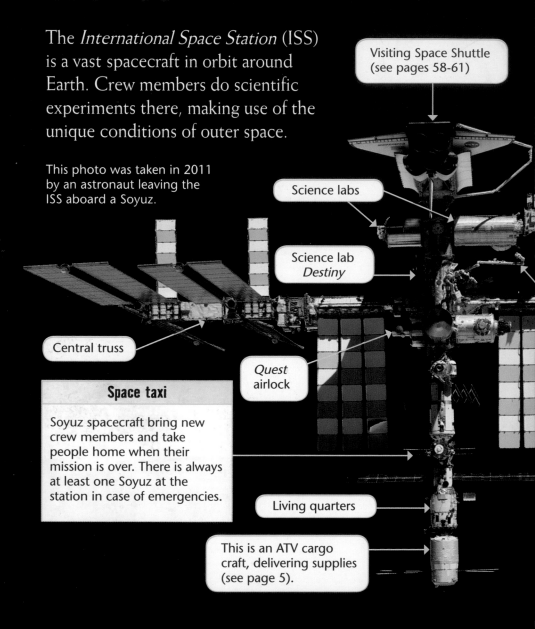

Visiting Space Shuttle (see pages 58-61)

Science labs

Science lab *Destiny*

Central truss

Quest airlock

Space taxi

Soyuz spacecraft bring new crew members and take people home when their mission is over. There is always at least one Soyuz at the station in case of emergencies.

Living quarters

This is an ATV cargo craft, delivering supplies (see page 5).

The US and Russia built most of the ISS. But lots of other countries were involved and crews from many different countries have visited the station.

Assembling the ISS

- The ISS took about 13 years to build.
- Each section, or module, was flown up separately from Earth.
- Astronauts have performed over 160 'spacewalks', spending over 1,000 hours working outside the ISS in spacesuits, doing repairs and construction work.

China wasn't involved in building the ISS and is creating its own space station instead. Chinese spacecraft that are similar to Soyuz craft will be used to carry crews.

The solar arrays gather energy from the Sun to power the ISS.

Robotic arm called *Canadarm2*

ISS (International, 1998–present)		Living quarters
• **Purpose:** orbital research facility where crews can live and work • **Crew:** up to six people at a time. The longest mission to the ISS was 215 days.	 57.5ft (109m)	• Two bathrooms • Gymnasium • Sleeping bags tethered to walls • Kitchen with table, oven and refrigerator

Docking in space

Once a Soyuz craft has been launched into space, its next step is to connect, or dock, with the ISS. It takes about two days and 34 orbits of the Earth for a Soyuz to get into exactly the right position to dock.

This is a Soyuz craft in orbit, approaching the ISS to dock.

The docking process is automatic, but the crew can take over if something goes wrong.

'Probe' docking mechanism. This is inserted into a cone-shaped 'drogue' on the ISS.

How a Soyuz docks with the ISS

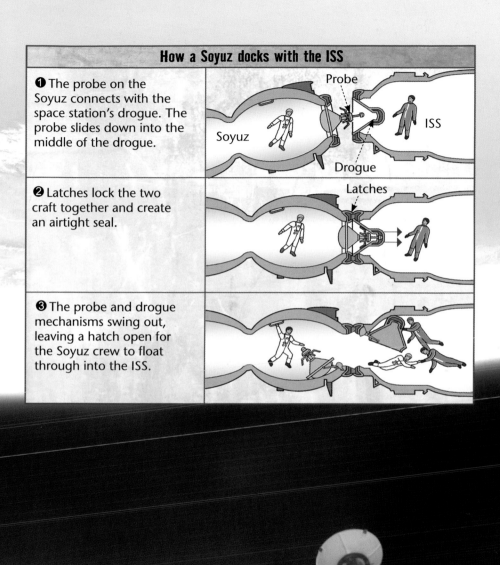

❶ The probe on the Soyuz connects with the space station's drogue. The probe slides down into the middle of the drogue.

Probe

Soyuz

ISS

Drogue

❷ Latches lock the two craft together and create an airtight seal.

Latches

❸ The probe and drogue mechanisms swing out, leaving a hatch open for the Soyuz crew to float through into the ISS.

The drogue is a funnel-shaped dip on the outside of the ISS. You can't see it properly here, but it's shown on the diagram above.

Floating around the ISS

In orbit, everything floats as though it's weightless. This is known as a zero-g environment. Every surface can be used to mount equipment and store supplies, since the floating crew can reach the ceiling as easily as the floor.

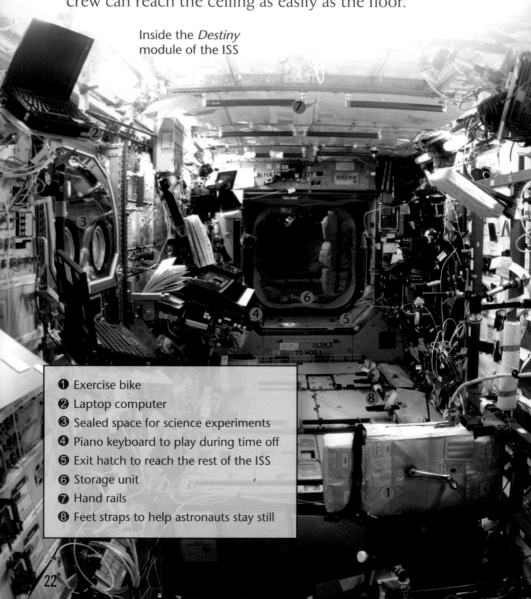

Inside the *Destiny* module of the ISS

❶ Exercise bike
❷ Laptop computer
❸ Sealed space for science experiments
❹ Piano keyboard to play during time off
❺ Exit hatch to reach the rest of the ISS
❻ Storage unit
❼ Hand rails
❽ Feet straps to help astronauts stay still

A typical day on board

06:00 Breakfast followed by exercise. The crew has to exercise for about two hours a day to stay healthy.

07:00 Taking a shower is tricky in zero-g. Instead of water, astronauts use shampoo wiped off with a towel.

08:00 The working day begins. This astronaut is doing minor repairs to the ISS's exterior.

13:00 Lunch. Sometimes, the ISS team can't resist using the zero g environment to play with their food.

19:30 Dinner and leisure time. This astronaut is playing chess with someone on Earth, via satellite linkup.

21:30 Bedtime. In orbit, you actually experience 16 dawns every 24 hours but the ISS crew sticks to a schedule that feels like an Earth day.

Floating experiments

Scientists use the zero-g environment of the ISS to do experiments that aren't possible on Earth. Many of these will help future astronauts to travel further into space.

Experimenting on astronauts

Many experiments on the ISS study how living in space affects the human body. Here are some questions scientists are trying to answer:

In space, people are exposed to lots of harmful **radiation** - the Earth's atmosphere usually protects us. How can astronauts protect themselves from this?

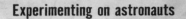

How does space travel affect an astronaut's sense of **balance**?

Muscle mass is lost when people spend time in zero g. Is it possible to stop this?

Bone loss is also a problem for astronauts. How can it be fought?

This scientist on the ISS is studying plant growth in zero-g. Learning how to grow food in space will be essential when humans travel to other planets.

Tank to give plants water and light

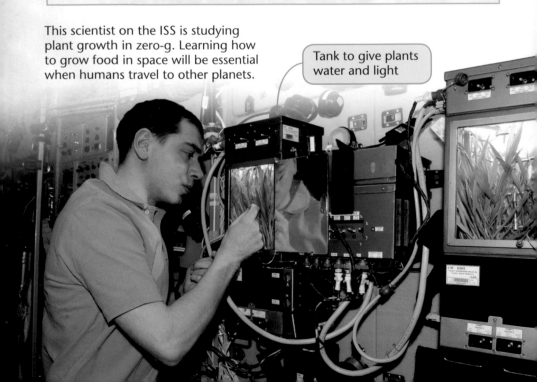

How Earth has gained from space science

- **New brain surgery techniques** based on robot arm and hand technology used on the ISS
- **Treatments for bone diseases** based on studies of bone loss in astronauts
- **Better understanding of climate change** by observing the planet from the outside
- **Invention of extra-strong materials** by mixing liquid metals in zero-g

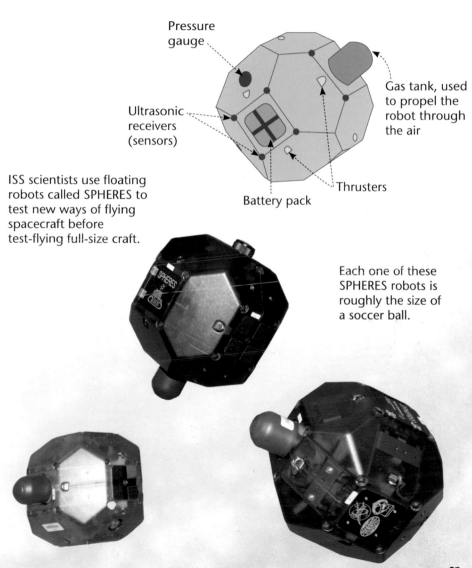

Pressure gauge

Gas tank, used to propel the robot through the air

Ultrasonic receivers (sensors)

Thrusters

Battery pack

ISS scientists use floating robots called SPHERES to test new ways of flying spacecraft before test-flying full-size craft.

Each one of these SPHERES robots is roughly the size of a soccer ball.

Spacesuits

When astronauts leave the ISS to go outside they have to wear special spacesuits. Each suit is like a mini spacecraft that keeps its wearer alive and safe in the harsh, airless conditions of space.

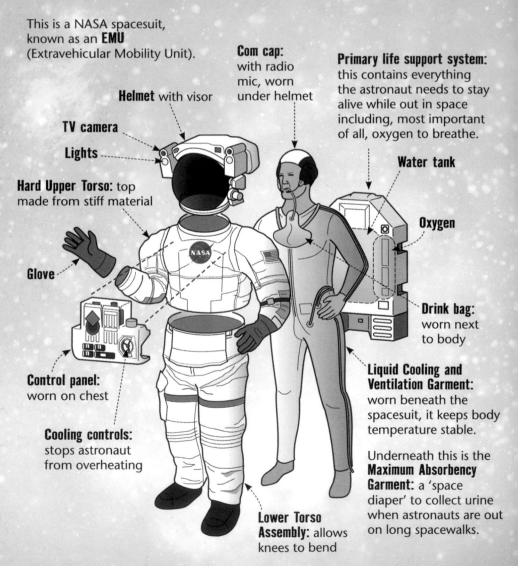

This is a NASA spacesuit, known as an **EMU** (Extravehicular Mobility Unit).

Com cap: with radio mic, worn under helmet

Primary life support system: this contains everything the astronaut needs to stay alive while out in space including, most important of all, oxygen to breathe.

Helmet with visor

TV camera

Lights

Water tank

Hard Upper Torso: top made from stiff material

Oxygen

Glove

Drink bag: worn next to body

Control panel: worn on chest

Cooling controls: stops astronaut from overheating

Liquid Cooling and Ventilation Garment: worn beneath the spacesuit, it keeps body temperature stable.

Underneath this is the **Maximum Absorbency Garment:** a 'space diaper' to collect urine when astronauts are out on long spacewalks.

Lower Torso Assembly: allows knees to bend

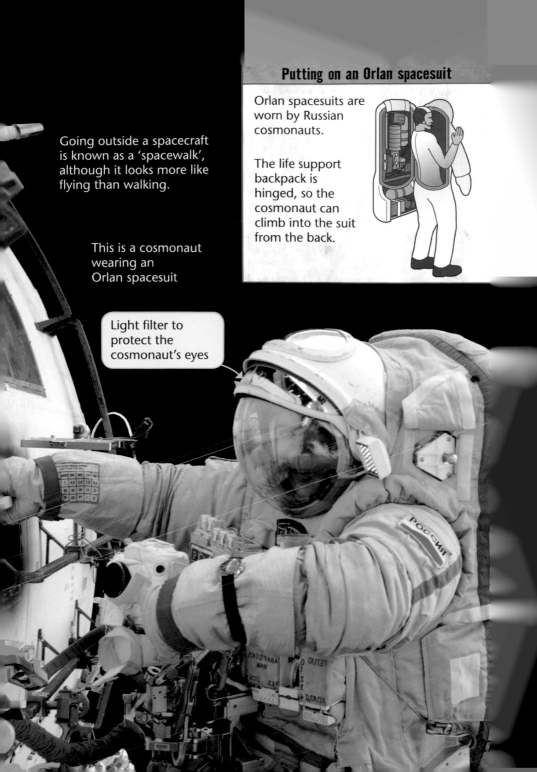

Going outside a spacecraft is known as a 'spacewalk', although it looks more like flying than walking.

This is a cosmonaut wearing an Orlan spacesuit

Putting on an Orlan spacesuit

Orlan spacesuits are worn by Russian cosmonauts.

The life support backpack is hinged, so the cosmonaut can climb into the suit from the back.

Light filter to protect the cosmonaut's eyes

Going outside

Before opening the outer hatch, astronauts and cosmonauts spend time in an airlock — a door compartment with two sections — while the air pressure is gradually reduced.

This is to prevent a potentially deadly condition called 'the bends'.

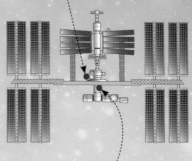

The *Quest* airlock shown in the photograph on the right is located here on the ISS.

Another airlock, called *Pirs*, is here.

How the airlock works

❶ Crew member puts on spacesuit in a section called the equipment lock. ❷ Hatch to ISS closed. ❸ Air pressure lowered slowly to match suit pressure by letting air out of the airlock.	Hatch leading from ISS	Equipment lock Crew lock Equipment lock hatch
❹ Crew member moves into crew lock area. ❺ The air pressure is reduced to zero, matching the airless environment outside.		Crew lock External hatch
❻ External hatch opens. ❼ Crew member floats out, attached to a tether to stop her or him from floating away.		Tether External hatch open

28

This astronaut is exiting the *Quest* airlock of the ISS.

A/L /05-04B

A/L /04-04B

Pistol Grip Tool

This is a multi-purpose power tool used on spacewalks.

Tether

Emergency jetpack

If the astronaut starts to drift, this can be used to steer back to the ISS and safety.

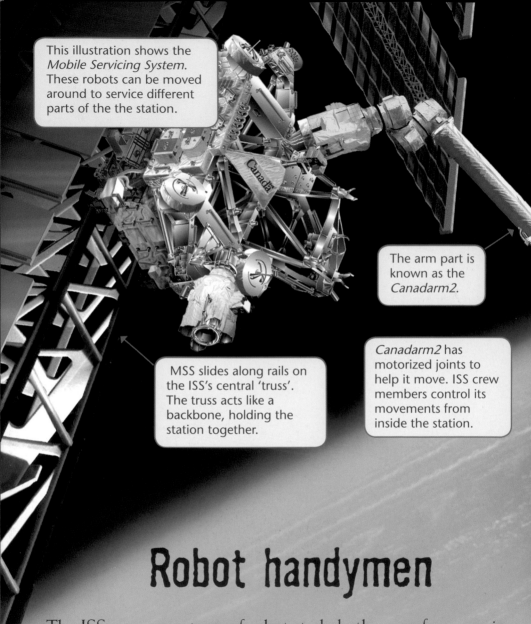

This illustration shows the *Mobile Servicing System*. These robots can be moved around to service different parts of the the station.

The arm part is known as the *Canadarm2*.

MSS slides along rails on the ISS's central 'truss'. The truss acts like a backbone, holding the station together.

Canadarm2 has motorized joints to help it move. ISS crew members control its movements from inside the station.

Robot handymen

The ISS crew use a team of robots to help them perform repairs, construction and other handy tasks outside the station. These robots can be programmed to do anything from fixing external cameras to helping spacecraft to dock by catching them.

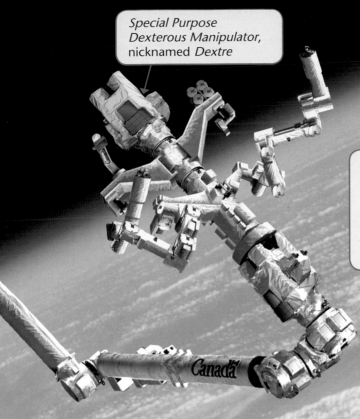

Special Purpose Dexterous Manipulator, nicknamed *Dextre*

Dextre is controlled from Earth, receiving commands from Mission Control. This is known as telemanipulation.

Robonaut 2

One robot on board the ISS is more human-like than the others: *Robonaut 2*. It was delivered to the station in February 2011 and is being tested in a lab on board.

It has video cameras for eyes.

Robonaut's touch-sensitive hands mean it can adjust its grip like a human and do jobs that *Dextre* (see above) can't.

The journey home

After a spacecraft leaves the ISS, it fires its engines to take it down out of orbit. This is known as a 'deorbit burn'. Earth's gravity then pulls the spacecraft down through the atmosphere at thousands of miles an hour. This is known as re-entry and it generates incredible heat.

These photographers are crowding around a Soyuz descent module after a successful landing.

The outside is scorched from the heat of re-entry.

Exit hatch for crew

Parachutes come out of here on the way down.

Re-entry and landing

When a Soyuz craft returns home, the crew sits inside the descent module. Heat shields protect them during re-entry, but the other modules are unshielded and burn up.

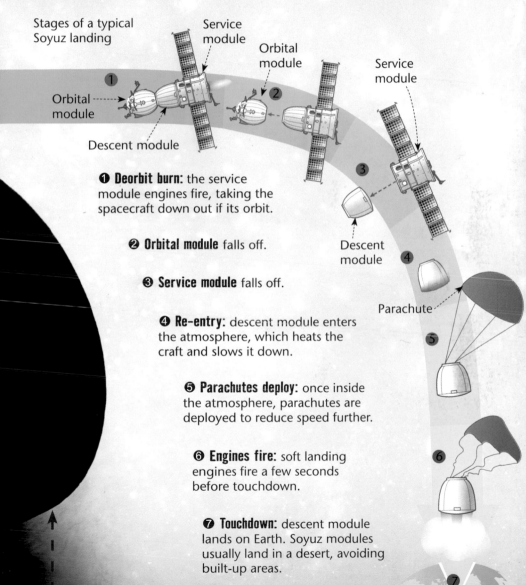

Stages of a typical Soyuz landing

Service module

Orbital module

Service module

① Orbital module

Descent module

②

③

④

⑤

⑥

Descent module

Parachute

❶ **Deorbit burn:** the service module engines fire, taking the spacecraft down out if its orbit.

❷ **Orbital module** falls off.

❸ **Service module** falls off.

❹ **Re-entry:** descent module enters the atmosphere, which heats the craft and slows it down.

❺ **Parachutes deploy:** once inside the atmosphere, parachutes are deployed to reduce speed further.

❻ **Engines fire:** soft landing engines fire a few seconds before touchdown.

❼ **Touchdown:** descent module lands on Earth. Soyuz modules usually land in a desert, avoiding built-up areas.

Space probes

Robotic craft known as space probes explore space, carrying cameras and other instruments. They use radio signals to send back data about other planets to Earth.

Some probes fly in orbit around planets. These are called orbital flights. Others fly past planets, known as a flyby.

This probe is very unusual because it came back to Earth after its mission.

Galileo (NASA, 1995 – 2003)

- **Flight type:** orbital, around Jupiter
- **Results:** found water on Europa, one of Jupiter's moons. This means that life might be possible there.

Hayabusa (Japan, 2003–2010)

- **Flight type:** return journey
- **Results:** collected a scraping of a space rock known as an asteroid, then flew back to Earth.

New Horizons (NASA, 2006–present)

- **Flight type:** flyby of Pluto, to take place in 2015
- **Aim:** to send back data about Pluto's structure.

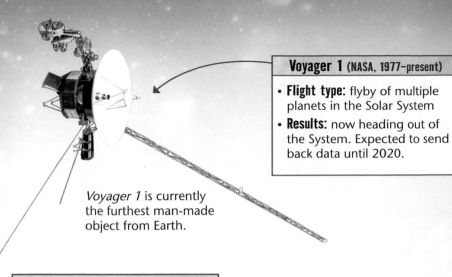

Voyager 1 (NASA, 1977–present)

- **Flight type:** flyby of multiple planets in the Solar System
- **Results:** now heading out of the System. Expected to send back data until 2020.

Voyager 1 is currently the furthest man-made object from Earth.

Messenger (NASA, 2004–present)

- **Flight type:** orbiting Mercury
- **Results:** discovered water in Mercury's atmosphere and various unexpected metals on the planet itself.

Cassini (NASA, 1997–present)

- **Flight type:** orbiting Saturn
- **Results:** sent back images and data about Saturn's rocky rings.

Exploring Mars

Two types of robots have landed on Mars: landers and rovers. Landers take images and do experiments without moving. Rovers roll around on wheels, so they can study a wider area.

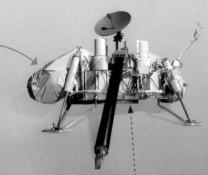

Viking 1 lander (NASA, 1975–82)

- **Launch vehicle:** Titan IIIE/Centaur
- **Mission:** to study Martian weather, rocks and soil, photograph the planet's surface and look for signs of life.

Instruments inside *Viking 1* did scientific experiments on Martian soil samples.

Phoenix lander (NASA, 2007–08)

- **Launch vehicle:** Delta II rocket
- **Mission:** to look for water and decide if the landing site could support life in the future, or did in the past.

This image of the surface of Mars was taken by *Opportunity*, one of two identical rover robots (see right).

Sojourner was the first Mars rover. It flew to Mars along with a lander.

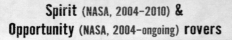

Sojourner rover (NASA, 1996–7)

- **Launch vehicle:** Delta II
- **Mission:** to study soil samples and test that rover technology worked before sending a more complex robot.

Spirit (NASA, 2004–2010) & Opportunity (NASA, 2004–ongoing) rovers

- **Launch vehicles:** Delta II (for both)
- **Mission:** to carry out detailed studies of soil and rock samples and photograph a wide area of the planet's surface.

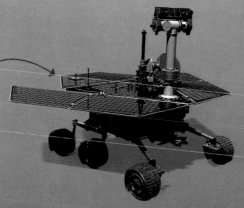

Curiosity rover

The latest rover, nicknamed *Curiosity*, is the size of a small car and is the most advanced robot rover yet. It was launched in November 2011.

This was the launch vehicle used to get *Curiosity* into space.

Atlas V launch vehicle

$\cdots$ 58m (190ft) $\cdots$

Enjoying a cruise

During its nine-month journey to Mars, *Curiosity* nestles inside a spacecraft made up of several different sections.

Spacecraft containing *Curiosity* rover

Cruise phase: contains thrusters which are used to make course corrections on the trip to Mars. These are jettisoned before landing.

Backshell: protects the rover in space and is jettisoned after entering the atmosphere of Mars.

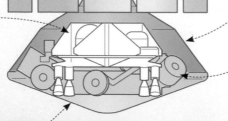

Descent stage: used for landing on Mars. It has thrusters to slow itself down before landing.

Rover

Heat shield: to slow down the spacecraft and protect the rover inside. This is jettisoned before landing.

Landing on Mars

During the final seconds before landing, *Curiosity* is lowered gently from the descent stage on a 'sky crane'.

This is an artist's impression of *Curiosity* just before landing on the surface of Mars.

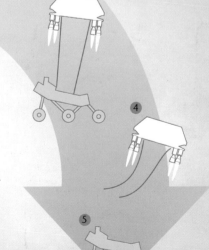

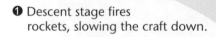

❶ Descent stage fires rockets, slowing the craft down.

❷ The rover is then lowered gently from the descent stage on cables, known as a sky crane.

❸ The rover's wheels come out of its body for touchdown.

❹ Sensors in the craft detect touchdown and the cables separate.

❺ The descent stage flies away and crash lands nearby.

A roving science lab

Curiosity's mission is to look for water and signs of life on Mars. The robot has multiple tools built into it to help it in its search.

The mast (rover's head) rises to about 2m (7ft) and houses cameras and other tools to scan the planet.

If *Curiosity's* landing goes smoothly, this is what it might look like when it's at work on the surface of Mars.

Mastcam is a camera that takes videos and images of the terrain.

Communications antenna

Each wheel has its own motor.

Curiosity rover 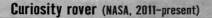 (NASA, 2011–present)

- **Purpose:** to study Mars and seek out water and life-forms.
- **Features:** Laser, six wheel drive, drilling arm, cameras
- **Launch vehicle:** Atlas V

A tool in the rover's 'head' called *ChemCam* fires a laser to blast pieces of rock into a mist, so *Curiosity* can study what they're made of.

A number of scientific tools are mounted on the rover's arm.

Curiosity is programmed from Earth. Each day's journey is planned out, then the instructions are beamed to it through space.

Early space travel

During the Second World War, the Germans built an exploding rocket weapon called the V-2. But scientists soon realized rocket technology could have a peaceful use: exploring space.

This is a V-2 rocket (also known as an A-4) on a launch pad in Germany in 1942.

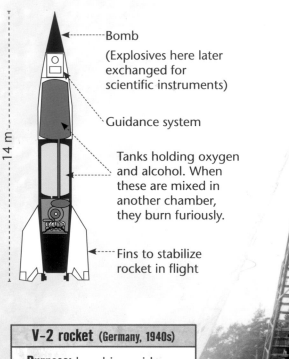

14 m

Bomb
(Explosives here later exchanged for scientific instruments)

Guidance system

Tanks holding oxygen and alcohol. When these are mixed in another chamber, they burn furiously.

Fins to stabilize rocket in flight

V-2 rocket (Germany, 1940s)

- **Purpose:** bombing raids and sending scientific instruments into space.
- **Range:** 206 km (128 miles) up. It could hit Earth targets as much as 300km (186 miles) away.

First craft in orbit

In the 1950s, scientists developed bigger, faster rockets. One of these, called an R-7 Sputnik, launched the first spacecraft to orbit Earth in 1957. The craft's name was *Sputnik 1*.

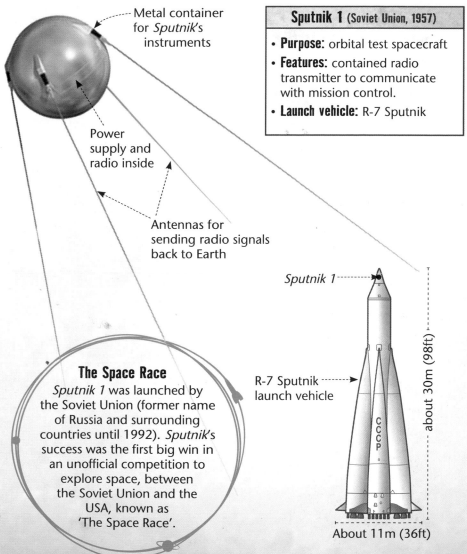

Metal container for *Sputnik*'s instruments

Power supply and radio inside

Antennas for sending radio signals back to Earth

Sputnik 1 (Soviet Union, 1957)

- **Purpose:** orbital test spacecraft
- **Features:** contained radio transmitter to communicate with mission control.
- **Launch vehicle:** R-7 Sputnik

Sputnik 1

R-7 Sputnik launch vehicle

about 30m (98ft)

About 11m (36ft)

The Space Race
Sputnik 1 was launched by the Soviet Union (former name of Russia and surrounding countries until 1992). *Sputnik*'s success was the first big win in an unofficial competition to explore space, between the Soviet Union and the USA, known as 'The Space Race'.

Animals in space

The first astronauts were animals, sent up to test how living things would react to the extreme conditions of space travel. Flies were sent up first, then mammals such as mice, monkeys and dogs.

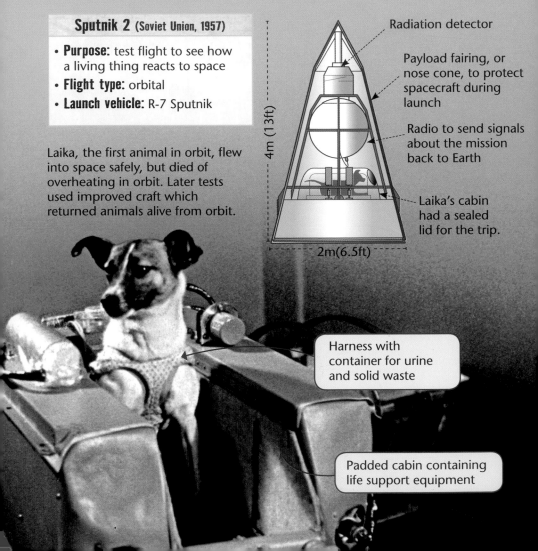

Sputnik 2 (Soviet Union, 1957)

- **Purpose:** test flight to see how a living thing reacts to space
- **Flight type:** orbital
- **Launch vehicle:** R-7 Sputnik

Laika, the first animal in orbit, flew into space safely, but died of overheating in orbit. Later tests used improved craft which returned animals alive from orbit.

4m (13ft)

2m(6.5ft)

Radiation detector

Payload fairing, or nose cone, to protect spacecraft during launch

Radio to send signals about the mission back to Earth

Laika's cabin had a sealed lid for the trip.

Harness with container for urine and solid waste

Padded cabin containing life support equipment

Flight of the space chimp

An American chimp-o-naut called Ham flew into space on January 31st 1961. He'd been trained to pull levers. But would he be able to perform these tasks while weightless? Ham was sent on a 16-minute flight to find out.

On launch day, NASA scientists applied sensors to Ham so they could monitor him in space.

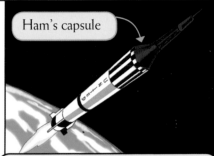

Ham's capsule

That afternoon, Ham was launched in a Mercury spacecraft on top of a Redstone launch vehicle.

It was a bumpy ride for Ham. But he performed well, pulling levers as he'd been trained to do.

His capsule splashed down safely. Doctors gave Ham a checkup. He was tired and dehydrated, but healthy.

More space beasts

- **Fruit flies** flew into space in a V-2 rocket in 1947. They survived.
- Two American-born **monkeys**, Able and Baker, flew into space and landed safely in 1959.
- In 1960, the first animals to orbit Earth and return safely were Belka and Strelka, a pair of Soviet **dogs**.
- The first **cat** flew into space from Algeria in Africa in 1963.

First man in space

In April 1961, Russian cosmonaut Yuri Gagarin became the first human being to fly into space. His spacecraft was called *Vostok 1.*

Gagarin in his flight suit and safety harness

After his craft re-entered the atmosphere, Gagarin ejected and parachuted back down to Earth from 7,000m (23,000ft).

❶ Cap worn under helmet
❷ Microphone
❸ Helmet with oxygen supply for emergencies
❹ Safety harness

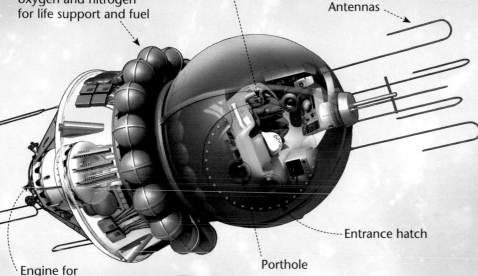

Vostok 1 after it was released from its launch vehicle. Part of the illustration has been cut away to show Yuri inside.

Spherical tanks holding oxygen and nitrogen for life support and fuel

Ejector seat to blast cosmonaut out for a parachute landing

Antennas

Entrance hatch

Porthole

Engine for braking on the way down

Scientists were worried that a human might panic in space. So *Vostok 1*'s controls were locked and the spacecraft was guided from Earth.

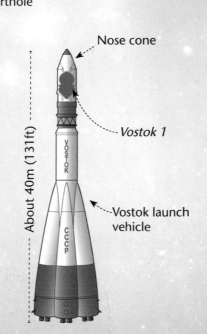

Nose cone

About 40m (131ft)

Vostok 1

Vostok launch vehicle

Vostok 1 (Soviet Union, 1961)

- **Launch vehicle**: Vostok
- **Purpose**: first human spaceflight
- **Flight type**: orbital

This is the launch of *Apollo 11*, the first manned Moon landing mission. The launch vehicle, a Saturn V, is still the biggest type of rocket ever built.

Crew spacecraft

Saturn V

Launch tower

47

The Apollo rocket

After its launch, each stage of *Apollo 11*'s Saturn V launch vehicle fired then dropped off. About three hours into the journey, the CSM flipped around, and connected nose-to-nose with the LM for the rest of the three-day trip to the Moon.

The same type of spacecraft and launch vehicle was used for all *Apollo* missions. There were five successful landings after *Apollo 11*.

This cut-away illustration shows *Apollo 11* and its Saturn V three stage launch vehicle. Saturn V rockets were used for all the *Apollo* missions, although not all the test flights carried a Lunar Module.

Five powerful engines to thrust rocket up from ground

Fuel tanks for first stage

Second stage powered by five engines

Fuel tanks for second stage

Third stage engine

Apollo 11 (NASA, 1969)

- **Launch vehicle:** Saturn V
- **Crew:** three astronauts
- **Purpose:** return trip to and landing on the Moon

This diagram shows how the stages of the launch vehicle dropped off and how the modules reached the Moon.

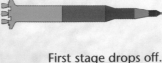

First stage drops off.

Second stage drops off.

To the Moon

During the 1960s and 1970s, NASA launched a series of missions called *Apollo* — their goal: to land on the Moon.

After some failures and test runs, three American astronauts blasted off in *Apollo 11* on July 16th, 1969. They were about to make history.

A guide to *Apollo 11* and its launch vehicle

The Saturn V launch vehicle was made up of three rocket stages.

Inside the nose was the crew spacecraft, made up of three parts:

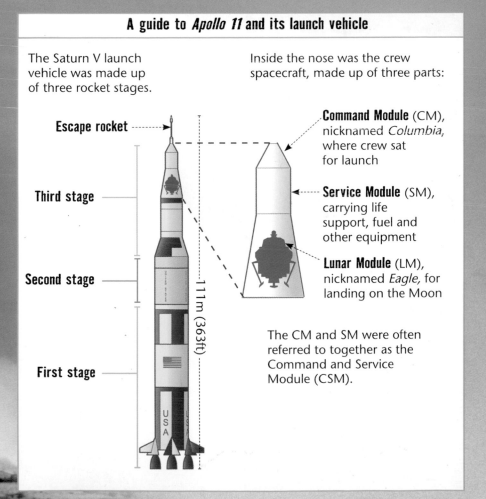

Escape rocket

Third stage

Second stage

First stage

111m (363ft)

USA

Command Module (CM), nicknamed *Columbia*, where crew sat for launch

Service Module (SM), carrying life support, fuel and other equipment

Lunar Module (LM), nicknamed *Eagle,* for landing on the Moon

The CM and SM were often referred to together as the Command and Service Module (CSM).

One small step 20th July 1969

Once in orbit around the Moon, *Eagle* separated from *Columbia* to perform the riskiest part of the mission so far: landing.

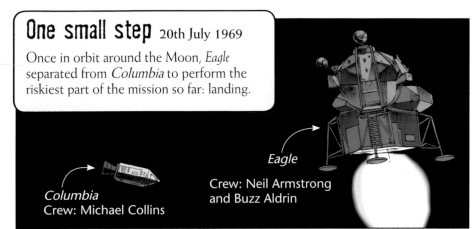

Columbia
Crew: Michael Collins

Eagle
Crew: Neil Armstrong and Buzz Aldrin

As *Eagle* descended, an alarm went off...

Program alarm!

Armstrong radioed Earth for advice. If the problem couldn't be fixed, they'd have to abort... when they were so close!

Roger, we got you...

Mission Control recognized what the alarm meant. They only had moments to decide what to do...

We're GO on that alarm.

Roger!

Mission Control decided it wasn't a serious problem and told the crew to go for landing.

The *Eagle* has Landed!

Down they flew until the *Eagle* touched down gently on the surface of the Moon. The crew got ready to climb down the ladder

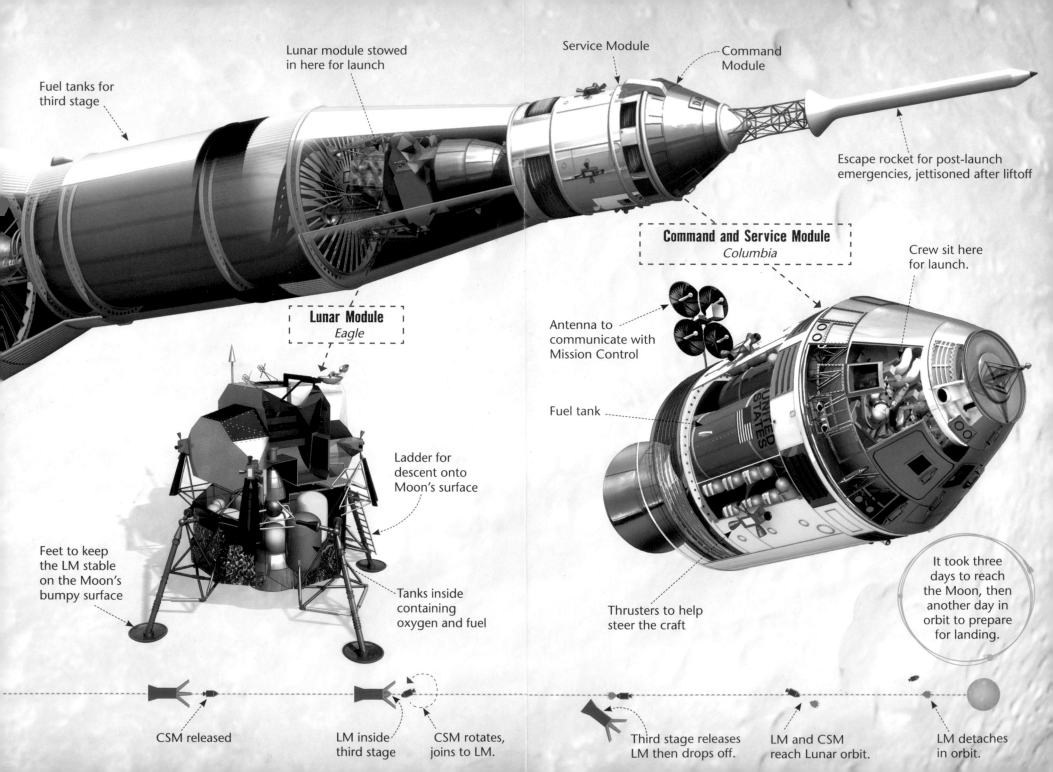

Fuel tanks for third stage

Lunar module stowed in here for launch

Service Module

Command Module

Escape rocket for post-launch emergencies, jettisoned after liftoff

Command and Service Module
Columbia

Crew sit here for launch.

Lunar Module
Eagle

Antenna to communicate with Mission Control

Ladder for descent onto Moon's surface

Fuel tank

Feet to keep the LM stable on the Moon's bumpy surface

Tanks inside containing oxygen and fuel

UNITED STATES

Thrusters to help steer the craft

It took three days to reach the Moon, then another day in orbit to prepare for landing.

CSM released

LM inside third stage

CSM rotates, joins to LM.

Third stage releases LM then drops off.

LM and CSM reach Lunar orbit.

LM detaches in orbit.

Back on Earth, millions of people watched Armstrong take his first bouncing steps on the Moon.

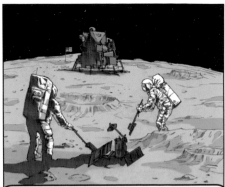

Aldrin soon joined him. Together they planted a US flag, gathered rock samples and did scientific experiments.

21 hours later, *Eagle* flew up to rejoin *Columbia*.

With Aldrin and Armstrong safely inside *Columbia*, the craft fired its engines, leaving the *Eagle* behind.

When they reached Earth, the crew were protected from the searing heat of re-entry by *Columbia*'s heat shield.

At last, the three men splashed down safely in the Pacific Ocean. *Apollo 11*'s mission had been a complete successs.

Men on the Moon

Armstrong and Aldrin spent 2½ hours on the Moon's surface. As well as setting up mechanical experiments and photographing their strange surroundings, they gathered about 21kg (46 lb) of rocks and dust for scientists to study back on Earth.

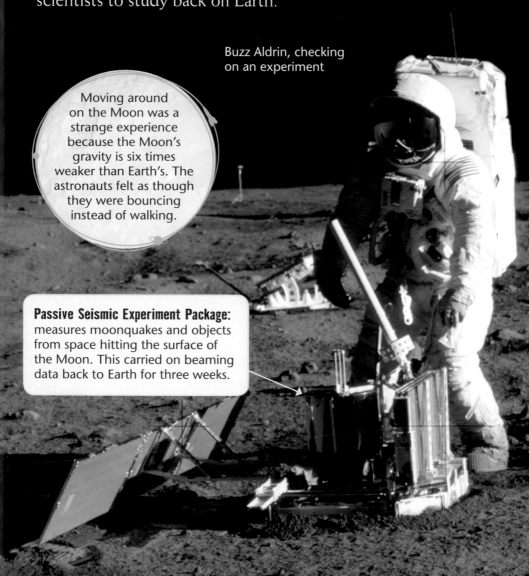

Buzz Aldrin, checking on an experiment

Moving around on the Moon was a strange experience because the Moon's gravity is six times weaker than Earth's. The astronauts felt as though they were bouncing instead of walking.

Passive Seismic Experiment Package: measures moonquakes and objects from space hitting the surface of the Moon. This carried on beaming data back to Earth for three weeks.

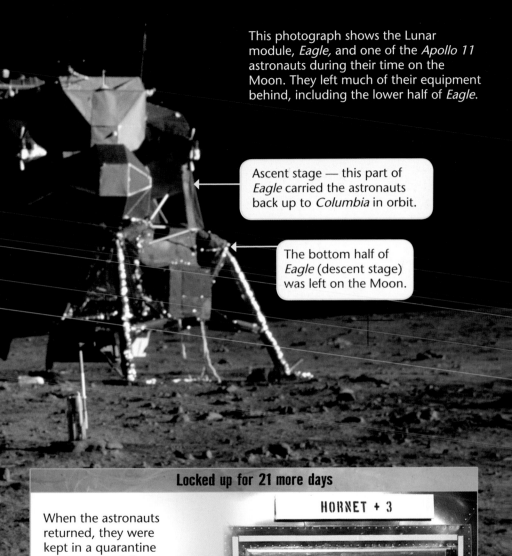

This photograph shows the Lunar module, *Eagle,* and one of the *Apollo 11* astronauts during their time on the Moon. They left much of their equipment behind, including the lower half of *Eagle*.

Ascent stage — this part of *Eagle* carried the astronauts back up to *Columbia* in orbit.

The bottom half of *Eagle* (descent stage) was left on the Moon.

Locked up for 21 more days

HORNET + 3

When the astronauts returned, they were kept in a quarantine unit — essentially a sealed caravan — in case they'd brought back any diseases. But scientists soon learned that no germs can live on the Moon.

Apollo 13 *April 13, 1970*

Like *Apollo 11*, *Apollo 12* was a success. When *Apollo 13* launched, the first few days of the trip went so smoothly that the ground crew even joked that they were bored. Until...

... an explosion ripped through *Apollo 13*'s Service Module.

Do you know what that noise was?

Inside the Command Module, the crew felt and heard the blast.

Houston, we've had a problem.

They radioed Mission Control for advice. Perhaps the craft could be fixed?

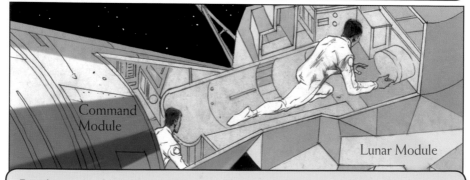

Command Module

Lunar Module

But the explosion had caused too much damage. The crew would have to use the Lunar Module (LM) as a lifeboat to get home.

The LM was only meant to keep *two* men alive for a two-day Moon landing. They did some calculations.

It seemed that their supplies would *just* last. On they went, steering around the Moon by firing the LM's engines.

As they hurtled Earthwards, the air filters began to fail.

The crew had to rig up a filter held together with plastic bags and sticky tape. They could breathe... but would their battered craft survive re-entry?

When the crew finally splashed down in the Pacific ocean, the men in Mission Control whooped with delight.

At last, the weary crew was safe, breathing the fresh sea air of Earth. They were home.

Moon buggy

After *Apollo 13*, all the *Apollo* missions were successful. The crews of *15, 16* and *17* used a Lunar Roving Vehicle (LRV). This meant they could cover more ground and carry more equipment than on foot.

Antenna for communicating with Earth and sending pictures back there

The LRV had a TV camera which could be operated from Mission Control on Earth.

Lunar Roving Vehicle (NASA, 1970s)

- **Purpose:** driving on the Moon
- **Top speed:** 13km/h (8mph)
- **Features:** camera, power steering giving a very tight turning radius, communication equipment

Each wheel could operate independently, so if any of them failed, the vehicle still worked.

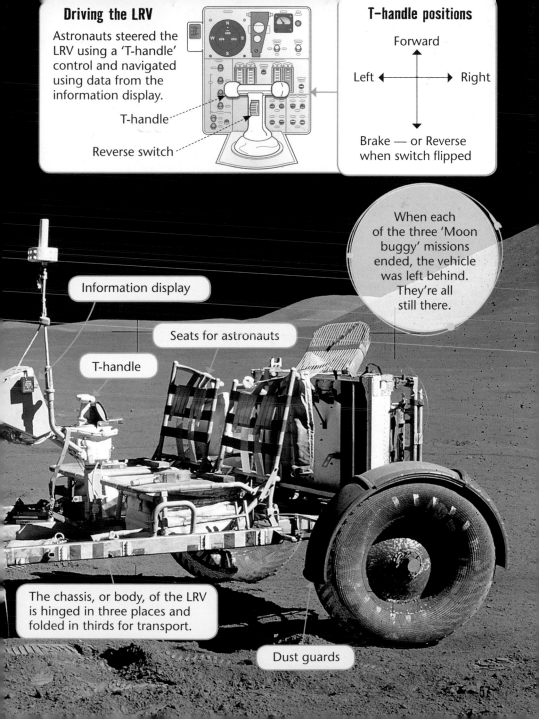

Driving the LRV

Astronauts steered the LRV using a 'T-handle' control and navigated using data from the information display.

T-handle

Reverse switch

T-handle positions

Forward

Left ← → Right

Brake — or Reverse when switch flipped

When each of the three 'Moon buggy' missions ended, the vehicle was left behind. They're all still there.

Information display

Seats for astronauts

T-handle

The chassis, or body, of the LRV is hinged in three places and folded in thirds for transport.

Dust guards

Space Shuttle

About ten years after the Moon landings, NASA introduced a new type of craft, the Space Shuttle. Shuttles were launched using rockets, but landed, like planes, on runways.

External fuel Tank (ET)

Solid Rocket Booster (SRB)

This part is known as the orbiter. It's a reusable spacecraft with a crew cabin and a large cargo bay.

Main engines: these draw fuel from the External fuel Tank.

United States

Discovery

A typical Shuttle flight

4 ET separation: orbiter continues into space alone.

5 Orbiter performs its mission, such as launching a satellite.

2 SRB separation: boosters drop off, main engines carry on firing.

3 SRBs splash down in the sea via parachutes.

6 Orbiter re-enters the atmosphere.

1 Liftoff: all rockets fire at once

7 Landing: orbiter glides to Earth. Parachutes open after touchdown.

Here Space Shuttle *Discovery* is being moved into position before launch.

The Shuttle's orbiter

NASA's Space Shuttles ferried astronauts and cargo to and from orbit. There were six in total, but one was only used for test flights. Each could stay in orbit for weeks at a time as free-flying spacecraft, or dock with the ISS — or with other, earlier, space stations.

Space Shuttle (NASA, 1981–2011)

- **Launch vehicle:** Solid Rocket Boosters (SRBs) with External fuel Tank (ET)
- **Orbiter function:** carrying cargo and astronauts to and from orbit

Approx 37m (122ft)

Approx 24m (78ft)

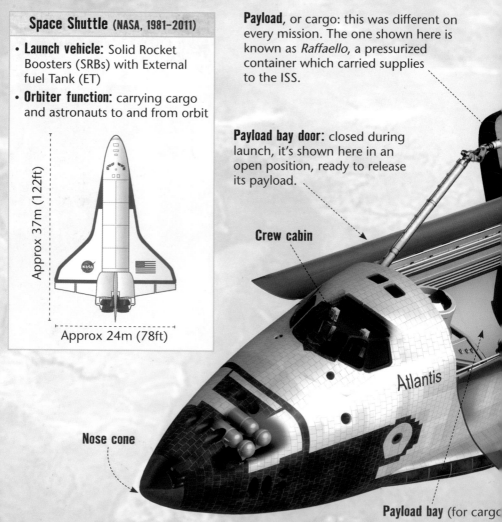

Payload, or cargo: this was different on every mission. The one shown here is known as *Raffaello*, a pressurized container which carried supplies to the ISS.

Payload bay door: closed during launch, it's shown here in an open position, ready to release its payload.

Crew cabin

Atlantis

Nose cone

Payload bay (for cargo

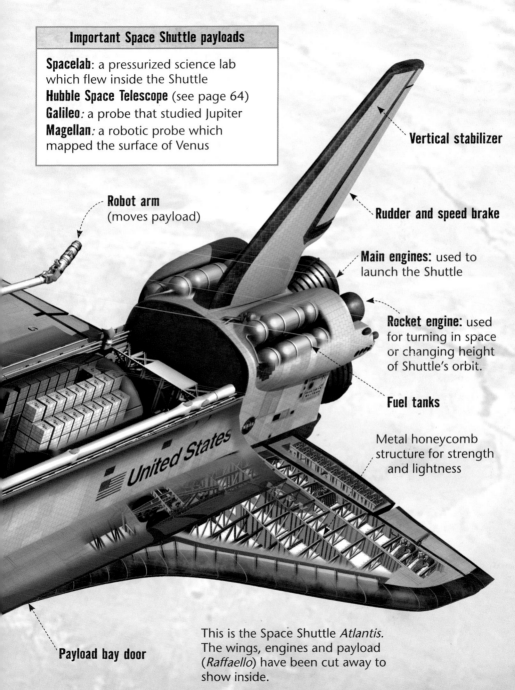

Robot arm
(moves payload)

Vertical stabilizer

Rudder and speed brake

Main engines: used to launch the Shuttle

Rocket engine: used for turning in space or changing height of Shuttle's orbit.

Fuel tanks

Metal honeycomb structure for strength and lightness

United States

Payload bay door

This is the Space Shuttle *Atlantis*. The wings, engines and payload (*Raffaello*) have been cut away to show inside.

Satellites

A satellite is an object in orbit around another object in space. Earth is a satellite of the Sun, for example. But around 16,000 artificial satellites have been sent into orbit around Earth, to do various different jobs.

This is an artist's impression of all Earth's satellites. Their size is exaggerated so you can see them. Some of the satellites in orbit around Earth are 'retired' (basically, not working any more). This 'space junk' can be dangerous for astronauts and spacecraft in orbit.

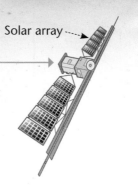

Solar array

Earth observation satellite

Used to photograph land, sea and weather, these satellites also use instruments such as x-rays to study the Earth's surface.

Broadcast and communications satellites

Used to bounce signals for TV, radio, telephones and internet from one point on Earth to another.

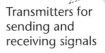

Transmitters for sending and receiving signals

Military satellites

Armies use satellites to spy on their enemies and to relay orders to troops in remote battle zones.

These military satellite dishes communicate with spy satellites in space.

Watchers in space

Some satellites gaze out at the Universe, taking photographs and gathering data. The *Hubble Space Telescope* is one of the most famous.

A telescope is a scientific instrument that people can use to see things that are incredibly far away.

Hubble Space Telescope
(NASA, 1990–present)

- **Mission:** photographing deep space.
- **Results:** *Hubble* data has helped scientists to estimate the age of the Universe.

This is a photograph of the Eagle Nebula, taken by *Hubble Space Telescope*. A nebula is a cloud of gas where stars are born.

Antenna for Earth communications

Door closed when Hubble is serviced to protect delicate instruments

Solar arrays to provide power

Kepler telescope
(NASA, 2009–present)

- **Mission:** to discover new planets outside the Solar System.
- **Results:** over 60 found so far with 1000s more waiting to be confirmed.

Artist's impression of *Kepler*

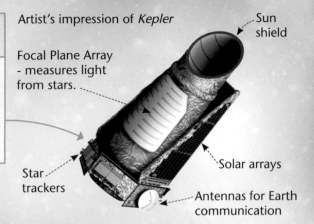

Sun shield

Focal Plane Array - measures light from stars.

Star trackers

Solar arrays

Antennas for Earth communication

This is an illustration of the *Solar Dynamics Observatory* (SDO), a robot lab in orbit around the Sun.

Antenna to send data to Earth

This box of instruments measures ultraviolet light.

Solar Dynamics Observatory
(NASA, 2010–present)

- **Mission:** to photograph and study the Sun.
- **Results:** greater understanding of how the Sun behaves and how it affects us on Earth.

Image of the Sun built up using data from the SDO

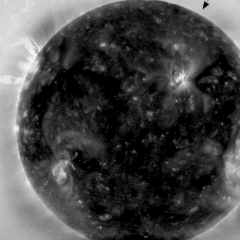

Solar panels to provide power

Cameras and telescopes

Box-shaped spacecraft that keeps telescope in orbit

65

A weightlessness training session inside a zero-gravity simulator, on board a Russian *IL-76 MDK* aircraft.

Training for space

Astronauts and cosmonauts have to train for years. As well as hours and hours in classrooms, studying hard, there is some very tough psychological and physical training involved.

Floating on a plane

Astronauts are trained using planes which fly up very fast and then down.

This leaves the passengers floating as though they're weightless for a short period. Also known as 'vomit comets', these planes can lead to nasty travel sickness.

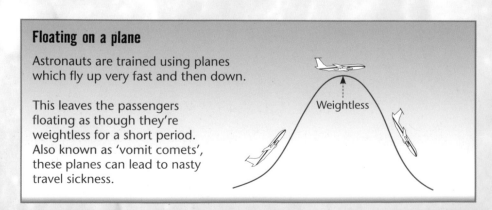

Weightless

Mars on Earth

In 2010, 6 cosmonauts went on a simulated Mars mission, at a base in Russia.

- **Duration:** 520 days
- **Crew:** 6 astonauts
- **Objective:** to test human mental and physical ability to cope with a long, cramped journey.

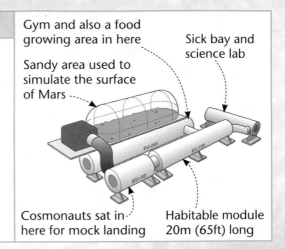

Gym and also a food growing area in here

Sick bay and science lab

Sandy area used to simulate the surface of Mars ---

Cosmonauts sat in here for mock landing

Habitable module 20m (65ft) long

Simulating zero-g in water

One of the ways that astronauts prepare for the zero-g environment of space is by training underwater. They have to get used to performing tasks when their bodies and other objects don't behave as they do in the air on Earth.

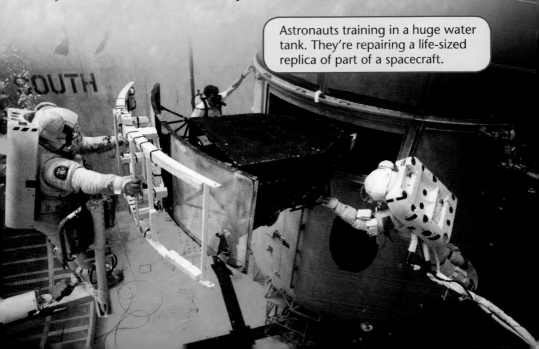

Astronauts training in a huge water tank. They're repairing a life-sized replica of part of a spacecraft.

Future space travel

NASA is developing a new craft to take crews to the ISS and beyond. But private companies such as SpaceX are also working on their own manned spacecraft.

Orion
(NASA, in testing phase)

- **Crew:** up to 4 astronauts
- **Launch vehicle:** to be confirmed

An uncrewed launch is planned for 2013, but it might be a while before crews take it for a test flight.

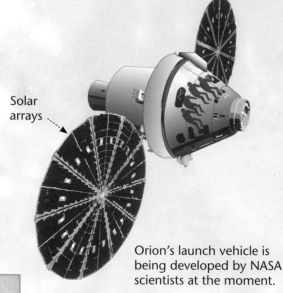

Solar arrays

Orion's launch vehicle is being developed by NASA scientists at the moment.

DragonRider
(SpaceX, manned launch planned 2014)

- **Crew:** up to 7 astronauts
- **Launch vehicle:** Falcon 9

An uncrewed version of the craft, called Dragon, was the first privately-owned spacecraft to dock with the ISS, in 2012.

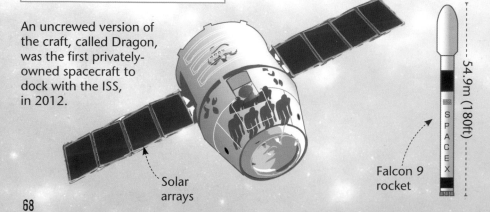

Solar arrays

54.9m (180ft)

SPACEX

Falcon 9 rocket

Launched from the air

Another company, Stratolaunch Sytems, plans to launch spacecraft from the air using a gigantic plane.

Stratolaunch aeroplane
(in development)

- **Secondary launch vehicle:** a 2-stage rocket
- **Payload:** could be used to launch either crewed craft or cargo vehicles into orbit

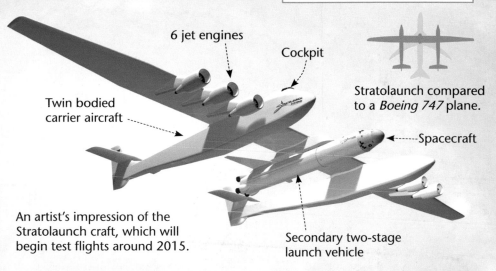

6 jet engines

Cockpit

Twin bodied carrier aircraft

Stratolaunch compared to a *Boeing 747* plane.

Spacecraft

An artist's impression of the Stratolaunch craft, which will begin test flights around 2015.

Secondary two-stage launch vehicle

How the Stratolaunch launch system works

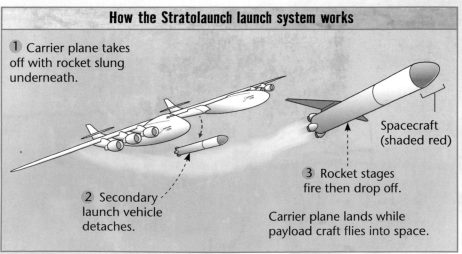

1 Carrier plane takes off with rocket slung underneath.

Spacecraft (shaded red)

3 Rocket stages fire then drop off.

2 Secondary launch vehicle detaches.

Carrier plane lands while payload craft flies into space.

Space tourists

Tourists have been flying into space on Russian and American craft since 2001.

The first purpose-built tourist craft is Virgin Galactic's *SpaceShipTwo*. Tickets are on sale now with first passenger launches planned for 2013 or 2014.

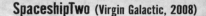

SpaceshipTwo (Virgin Galactic, 2008)

- **Launch vehicle:** *WhiteKnightTwo* plus the spacecraft's own engines
- **Capacity:** 6 passengers, 2 pilots
- **Purpose:** pleasure trips to space and zero-g science experiments

Artist's impression of the planned stages of *SpaceShipTwo*'s journey into space.

4 Passengers will experience zero-g for a few minutes. Wings raised to prepare for re-entry.

SpaceShipTwo will be launched by 'mothership' aircraft, *WhiteKnightTwo*.

3 Engines cut out and craft reaches space.

2 Rocket engines fire.

1 *SpaceShipTwo* launched from the air.

At the end of the trip, the craft will glide down to Earth, tugged by gravity.

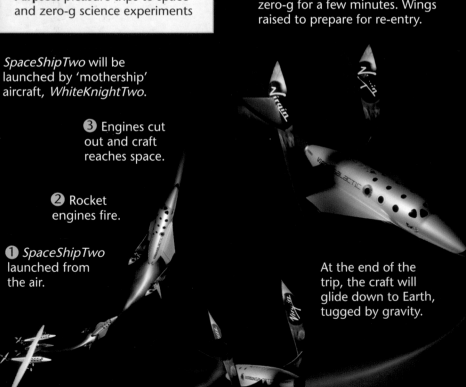

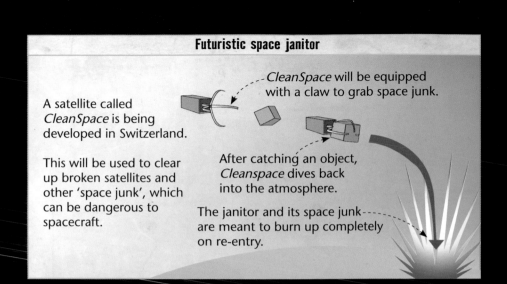

Futuristic space janitor

A satellite called *CleanSpace* is being developed in Switzerland.

This will be used to clear up broken satellites and other 'space junk', which can be dangerous to spacecraft.

CleanSpace will be equipped with a claw to grab space junk.

After catching an object, *Cleanspace* dives back into the atmosphere.

The janitor and its space junk are meant to burn up completely on re-entry.

Expandable space station

Another space company, Bigelow Aerospace, is planning an expandable space station. Air will be pumped into the station to inflate it once each piece is in orbit.

Bigelow's space station is made of a tough material also used in bomb protection gear.

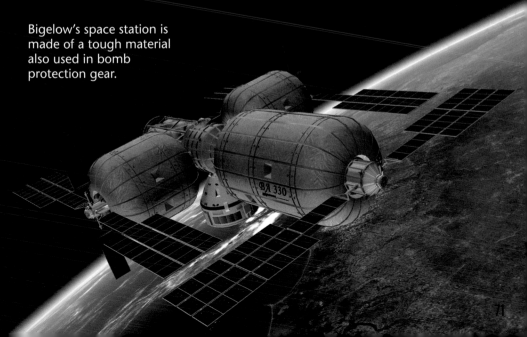

Spacecraft over time

110 m

This line-up shows launch vehicles and spacecraft featured in this book.

The Saturn V launch vehicle, which carried astronauts on the *Apollo* Moon missions, is still the largest type of launch vehicle ever used.

50 m

Vostok 1's launch vehicle was taller than the Statue of Liberty.

Eagle
1969

Voyager 1
1977

Vostok 1
1961

Sputnik 1
1957

0 m

V2 Rocket	Sputnik	Vostok	Saturn V	Titan IIIE/Centaur
1940s	1957–8	1960s	1967–1973	1974–77

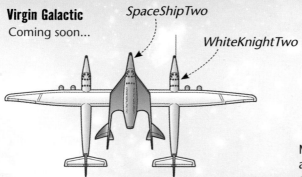

Virgin Galactic
Coming soon...

SpaceShipTwo

WhiteKnightTwo

Many of these launch vehicles are capable of carrying different types of spacecraft.

The Space Shuttle's orbiter plays a part in the launch process, firing its engines, so it's both a spacecraft and part of the launch vehicle.

Curiosity rover
2012

Dragon
2012

Soyuz

Satellites

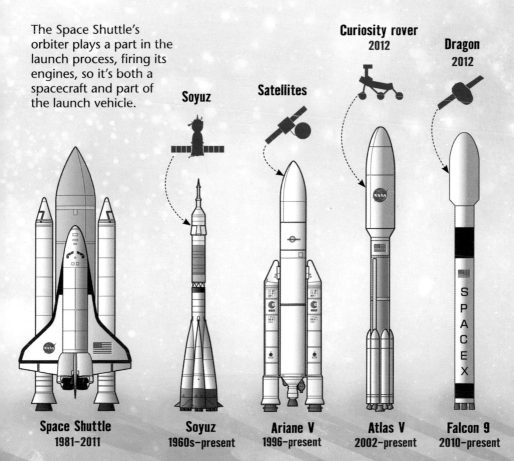

Space Shuttle
1981–2011

Soyuz
1960s–present

Ariane V
1996–present

Atlas V
2002–present

Falcon 9
2010–present

Space on the internet

There are lots of websites with information about spacecraft. At the Usborne Quicklinks Website, you'll find links to some great sites where you can:

• Watch video clips of rocket launches.
• See inside the International Space Station.
• Get updates on the latest space missions and discoveries.
• See dramatic images captured by space telescopes.

For links to recommended websites, go to **www.usborne-quicklinks.com** and enter the keyword **space**.

When using the internet please follow the internet safety guidelines displayed on the Usborne Quicklinks Website. The websites in Usborne Quicklinks are regularly reviewed and updated, but Usborne Publishing Ltd is not responsible for the content or availability of any website other than its own. We recommend that children are supervised while using the internet.

Want to be an astronaut?

Working in space is difficult and dangerous and takes years of training. Even before training begins, astronauts and cosmonauts have to...

❶ Do very well at school, especially in science and mathematics, then get a university degree.

❷ Have good enough social skills to spend every waking hour with other people inside a cramped spacecraft.

❸ Be incredibly physically fit.

❹ Be no shorter than 157.5 (5ft2) and no taller than 190.5 cm (6ft3), as spacecraft are snug, but you need to be able to reach the controls.

Find out more on the Usborne Quicklinks Website...

A Falcon 9 launch vehicle and Dragon spacecraft taking off, carrying supplies to the ISS

For links to websites about space and spacecraft, go to the Usborne Quicklinks Website at **www.usborne-quicklinks.com** and enter the keyword **space**.

Glossary

This glossary explains some of the words used in this book. If a word is written in *italic* type, it has an entry of its own.

airlock A door made up of several chambers that leads into (and out of) space, found on a *space station*.

antenna A device used to send and receive radio signals across space.

asteroid A small, rocky or metallic object orbiting the Sun.

astronaut A professional space voyager, often a trained scientist.

atmosphere Layer of gases surrounding a planet.

cosmonaut A professional space voyager, often a scientist, employed by the Russian *space agency*.

docking When one *spacecraft* connects with another in space.

EMU A type of *spacesuit*. Stands for Extra Vehicular Mobility Unit.

Flight Director The person in *Mission Control* who gives the orders during a space *mission*.

flyby A word used to describe the flight of a *probe* or other *spacecraft* past a planet or other body in space.

gravity A pulling force that stops you from floating into space when you're on Earth. All planets and other large objects in space have their own gravity that pulls on other objects.

heat shield The part of a spacecraft that protects it during *re-entry*.

Karman Line The place, 100km (62 miles) up from Earth, often used as the boundary between Earth's *atmosphere* and outer space begins.

lander A type of robotic *spacecraft* carrying scientific instruments that lands on alien worlds to study them.

launch vehicle A *rocket*-powered vehicle used to carry *spacecraft* from Earth to space, falling away afterwards.

liftoff The moment when a *spacecraft* takes off from the ground.

Lunar Roving Vehicle A car-like vehicle used by *astronauts* to drive around on the Moon.

manned When a *spacecraft* carries people, it is known as a manned (or sometimes crewed) spacecraft.

mission A journey into space with a particular goal. Missions can be either *manned* or *unmanned*.

Mission Control A room on Earth where engineers and other ground support staff sit to monitor a *spacecraft*'s progress and relay orders to the crew or send commands to robot *spacecraft*.

module A section of a *spacecraft* or *space station*.

moon A large rocky or icy object in orbit around a planet.

orbiting Moving in an oval or circular pattern around a planet or other large space object. Orbiting objects are said to be 'in orbit'.

orbiter (Space Shuttle) The plane-like part of the *Space Shuttle*, which has a crew cabin and a *payload* bay.

Orlan A type of *spacesuit* used by *cosmonauts*.

payload Cargo carried into space. A payload is often a *spacecraft* in its own right, such as a *satellite*.

payload bay The area of a *spacecraft*, such as the *Space Shuttle*, that is used to carry the *payload*.

payload fairing Also known as a nose cone, this is a protective covering at the tip of a *launch vehicle*, housing the *spacecraft*.

probe (spacecraft) A robotic *spacecraft* carrying scientific exploration of solar system done by probes

probe and drogue (mechanism) Two-part mechanism used for *docking*.

re-entry When a *spacecraft* returns from space into the *atmosphere*. This generates incredible heat.

rocket (engine) A device that uses burning fuel to push *launch vehicles* into the air and to help *spacecraft* navigate through space.

rover A wheeled robot designed to explore the surface of an alien world, carrying scientific equipment.

satellite An object in orbit around a planet, moon or star. Usually refers to an artificial satellite, an *orbiting* machine used for communications, broadcast, or observation.

space agency A government organization in charge of running and paying for space *missions* and *spacecraft*.

Space Shuttle A type of *spacecraft* with a plane-like orbiter used from 1981-2011 to carry *astronauts* and *payloads* into orbit.

space station A *spacecraft* that remains in orbit for years. It acts as a base where *astronauts* and *cosmonauts* live and perform scientific experiments.

space tourist Someone who pays to travel into space.

spacecraft A vehicle that travels in space.

spacesuit A sealed suit with its own oxygen supply and various layers of protection which protects *astronauts* or *cosmonauts* on s*pacewalks*.

spacewalk Time spent outside a *spacecraft* or *space station*.

unmanned Describes a *spacecraft* or space *mission* that has no crew.

zero-g Experienced when a *spacecraft* is flying in orbit. In zero-g, objects and passengers float around.

Index

Page numbers marked with an 'a' are underneath the flap on that page. Words in *italics* are names of spacecraft, robots or modules.

Acknowledgements

Every effort has been made to trace and acknowledge ownership of copyright. If any rights have been omitted, the publishers offer to rectify this in any future editions following notification. The publishers are grateful to the following individuals and organizations for permission to reproduce material on the following pages: (t=top, b=bottom, r=right, l=left)

cover Artist's impression of the Orion spacecraft flying to the Moon and background © Lockheed Martin Corporation and NASA, Close-Up of Earth © VGL/amanaimages/Corbis, Jupiter © William Radcliffe/Science Faction/Corbis, Mars © NASA **p1** SpaceX Dragon spacecraft attached to *Canadarm2* © NASA; **p2-3** Astronauts working on the *International Space Station* © NASA; **p4-5** © David Ducros/SPL; **p6-7** © NASA; **p8-9** Photo © NASA/NOAA/GSFC/Suomi/NPP/VIIRS/Norman Kuring, illustration © Adrian Roots; **p8a-9a** Sun © Denis Scott/CORBIS, planets image © William Radcliffe/Science Faction/Corbis, Ganymede image © NASA, Cassini image © NASA/JPL; *Voyager 1* image © NASA/JPL; **p10 -11** Photo © NASA/Bill Ingalls; **p12-13** Large Soyuz spacecraft © John Fox, small Soyuz diagram © Adrian Roots **p14-15** Illustrations © Adrian Roots, photo © NASA/Bill Ingalls; **p16-17** Photo © NASA; **p18-19** © NASA/Paolo Nespoli; **p20-21** Photo © NASA, illustration © Adrian Roots; **p22** © NASA; **p23** Picture strip © Paul Davidson; **p24-25** © NASA; **p26** © Adrian Roots; **p27 (tr)** © Adrian Roots, **(b)** NASA; **p28** © Adrian Roots; **p29** © NASA; **p30-31** Illustration © MDA; **p31** Photo © NASA; **p32** Photo © NASA/Bill Ingalls; **p33** Illustration © Adrian Roots; **p34** *Hayabusa* image © JAXA/Akihito Ikeshita, *Galileo* image © NASA/JPL-Caltech, *New Horizons* image © NASA/ JHUAPL/SwRI; **p35** *Voyager 1* image © NASA/JPL, *Messenger* image © NASA/JHUAPL/CIW, *Cassini* image © NASA/JPL; **p36-37** Photo of Mars © NASA/JPL/Cornell University *Viking 1* image © NASA/JPL-Caltech/ University of Arizona, *Phoenix* image © NASA/JPL, *Sojourner* image © NASA/JPL-Caltech, *Spirit/Opportunity* image © NASA/JPL; **p38** © Adrian Roots; **p39 (t)** © NASA/JPL-Caltech **(b)** © Adrian Roots; **p40-41** © NASA/JPL/Cornell University; **p42** Illustration © Adrian Roots, V-2 photo © DETLEV VAN RAVENSWAAY/ SPL; **p43** © Stephen Sweet/Alamy, **(br)** © Adrian Roots; **p44 (tr)** © Adrian Roots **(bl)** © RIA Novosti/Alamy; **p45** Picture strip © Paul Davidson; **p46** © RIA Novosti/SPL; **p47 (t)** John Fox, **(br)** © Adrian Roots; **p48** © NASA; **p49** © Adrian Roots; **p48a-49a** (under the flaps) All © John Fox; **p50-51** © Paul Davidson; **p52-53** All © NASA; **p54-55** Picture strip © Paul Davidson; **p56-57** © Corbis, **(t)** © Adrian Roots, **p58-59 photo** © Larry Tanner, 2010, **p59 (t)** © Adrian Roots; **p60 (l)** © Adrian Roots; **p60-61** Large orbiter illustration © John Fox; **p62** Debris objects in low-Earth Orbit © ESA; **p63 (t)** © Adrian Roots, **(b)** © U.S. Army/Mary Hogle; **p64** Illustration of HST © PAUL WOOTON/SPL, **(bl)** Image of Eagle Nebula taken by HST © NASA, ESA and The Hubble Heritage Team; **p65 (t)** *Kepler* image © LYNETTE COOK/SPL, **(bl)** © PAUL WOOTON, **(br)** © NASA/Goddard/SDO AIA Team; **p66 (t)** © Maxim Marmur/AFP/Getty Images; **p67 (t)** Adrian Roots, **(b)** © Corbis; **p69 (t)** Courtesy of Stratolaunch Systems **(b)** © Adrian Roots; **p70** © Virgin Galactic; **p71** © Courtesy of Bigelow Aerospace; **p72-73** © Adrian Roots; **p74-75** © SpaceX

Series editor: Jane Chisholm   Series designer: Zoe Wray
Picture research: Ruth King   Digital design: John Russell
With special thanks to Ed Van Cise and Scott Maxwell at NASA
and Michelle Jackley and Stephen Attenborough at Virgin Galactic.